Table Of Contents

Chapter 2: Historical Footprints 1

Chapter 3: Architectural Wonders 1

Chapter 4: The Flamenco Spirit 1

Chapter 5: Culinary Journeys 1

Chapter 6: Festivals and Celebrations 1

Chapter 7: Natural Landscapes 1

Chapter 8: Cities of Andalusia 1

Chapter 9: Spiritual Journeys 1

Chapter 10: Modern Andalusia 1

Chapter 1: The Allure of Andalusia 1

Chapter 1: The Allure of Andalusia

The Geography of Andalusia

Andalusia, located in the southernmost region of Spain, boasts a diverse geography that greatly influences its climate, culture, and lifestyle. This region is characterized by a mix of coastal plains, rolling hills, and rugged mountain ranges, creating a tapestry of landscapes that invite exploration. The Mediterranean Sea borders the southern edge, providing a warm and inviting climate that contributes to Andalusia's agricultural bounty, particularly its olives and citrus fruits. The interplay between the sea and the land creates a unique environment that has shaped the lives of its inhabitants for centuries.

The Sierra Nevada mountain range, home to the highest peaks in mainland Spain, stands as a prominent feature of Andalusia's geography. This majestic range not only provides stunning vistas but also plays a crucial role in the local climate. The mountains capture moisture from incoming weather systems, resulting in a diverse ecosystem that supports unique flora and fauna. The influence of the Sierra Nevada extends to the Alhambra in Granada, where the dramatic backdrop of the mountains enhances the historical significance of this UNESCO World Heritage site. Travelers can enjoy hiking and skiing in the Sierra Nevada, making it a year-round destination for outdoor enthusiasts.

In contrast to the mountainous areas, the Guadalquivir River flows through the heart of Andalusia, shaping the fertile plains that surround it. This river has historically been a lifeline for trade and agriculture, allowing cities such as Seville and Córdoba to flourish. The surrounding landscape, rich in alluvial soil, supports extensive farming and has made the region known as "the breadbasket of Spain." The riverbanks are dotted with charming whitewashed villages and historic towns, each offering a glimpse into the rich cultural tapestry of Andalusia. Exploring these areas provides travelers with a sense of the region's agricultural heritage and the importance of the river in shaping its history.

The coast of Andalusia is equally captivating, featuring a blend of sandy beaches and rugged cliffs that attract sun-seekers and adventure lovers alike. The Costa del Sol, with its sunny disposition, has long been a favorite among tourists, offering a vibrant atmosphere filled with beach clubs, restaurants, and nightlife. In contrast, the Costa de la Luz, known for its natural beauty and less commercialized beaches, appeals to those seeking a more tranquil experience. The coastal geography not only supports tourism but also plays a vital role in the region's fishing industry, which remains a crucial part of local economies and culinary traditions.

Andalusia's geography is further enriched by its varied microclimates, which contribute to the region's agricultural diversity. From the arid landscapes of Almeria to the lush valleys of Ronda, each area offers unique produce and local specialties. The distinct climate zones make Andalusia a paradise for food lovers, showcasing a wide range of flavors and culinary traditions that reflect the land's bounty. Travelers exploring Andalusia's geography will find that the interplay between landscape and lifestyle creates an authentic experience, allowing them to connect deeply with the soul of this remarkable region.

A Tapestry of Cultures

Andalusia, a region steeped in history, is a vivid tapestry of cultures woven together over centuries. The influences of various civilizations are evident in its architecture, art, music, and traditions. From the Phoenicians and Romans to the Moors and Christians, each group has left an indelible mark on the cultural landscape, creating a unique blend that defines the essence of Andalusia today. Travelers are invited to explore this rich heritage, where every corner tells a story and every monument holds a piece of history.

The architectural marvels of Andalusia reflect its multifaceted history. The Alhambra in Granada serves as a stunning example of Moorish architecture, showcasing intricate tile work, serene gardens, and majestic palaces. Meanwhile, the Great Mosque of Córdoba stands as a testament to the Islamic Golden Age, featuring a forest of columns and arches that mesmerize visitors. In contrast, the Gothic cathedrals of Seville and Cádiz illustrate the later Christian influence, demonstrating a shift in artistic expression and cultural priorities. Each site is not merely a structure but a narrative of coexistence and conflict among diverse cultures.

The culinary landscape of Andalusia further exemplifies this cultural fusion. The region's gastronomy is a delightful blend of flavors and techniques, influenced by the agricultural traditions of its various inhabitants. Dishes such as gazpacho and paella highlight the use of fresh local ingredients, showcasing the Mediterranean diet enriched by North African spices and the agricultural practices of the Romans. Travelers can indulge in tapas, an emblematic culinary tradition that encourages sharing and community, reflecting the social fabric of Andalusian life.

Music and dance also serve as vital expressions of Andalusian culture, deeply rooted in its diverse history. Flamenco, with its passionate rhythms and emotive storytelling, embodies the spirit of the region. While its origins can be traced back to the Romani people and Moorish influences, flamenco has evolved into a vibrant art form that captivates audiences worldwide. Festivals celebrating this cultural phenomenon, such as the Bienal de Flamenco in Seville, offer travelers a chance to experience the heart and soul of Andalusian tradition through live performances.

The vibrant communities of Andalusia continue to celebrate their rich heritage, fostering a sense of identity that is both historical and contemporary. Local festivals, such as La Feria de Abril in Seville and the Semana Santa processions, bring together people from different backgrounds, showcasing the unity and diversity that define the region. As travelers navigate through the streets of Andalusia, they will find that the past is not a distant memory but a living, breathing part of everyday life, inviting them to be a part of this intricate tapestry of cultures.

The Role of Nature in Andalusian Identity

The landscape of Andalusia is more than just a backdrop; it is a vital component of the region's identity. The diverse topography, which includes mountains, plains, and coastlines, shapes the customs, traditions, and lifestyles of its inhabitants. From the Sierra Nevada's snow-capped peaks to the sun-drenched beaches of the Costa del Sol, nature influences not only the way people interact with their environment but also how they perceive themselves. The interplay between the land and its people creates a unique cultural tapestry that travelers can explore, revealing the deep connections between nature and Andalusian identity.

Agriculture plays a significant role in this relationship with the land. The fertile plains of the Guadalquivir River valley have supported generations of farmers, fostering a culture deeply rooted in the rhythms of the seasons. Traditional crops such as olives, grapes, and citrus fruits are not just staples of the Andalusian diet; they also symbolize the region's historical ties to the earth. Travelers can witness this connection in local markets, where fresh produce reflects the vibrant landscapes of Andalusia. The act of harvesting and celebrating these crops during festivals further emphasizes the community's bond with nature.

The natural beauty of Andalusia has also inspired a rich artistic heritage. From the intricate tile work of Moorish architecture to the flamenco rhythms that echo the sounds of the countryside, nature serves as a muse for artists, musicians, and writers. The passionate landscape of Andalusia is captured in the works of renowned figures such as Federico García Lorca, whose poetry often reflects the deep emotional ties to the surrounding environment. For travelers, engaging with this artistic legacy provides a deeper understanding of how nature is woven into the fabric of Andalusian culture.

Furthermore, the diverse ecosystems of Andalusia contribute to the region's biodiversity, which is celebrated and preserved by local communities. The Sierra de Grazalema and Doñana National Parks, among others, are vital habitats for numerous species, showcasing the importance of conservation efforts. Travelers interested in ecotourism have the opportunity to explore these natural wonders, participating in activities that promote environmental awareness and sustainability. This connection to nature not only enhances the travel experience but also reinforces the significance of preserving the landscapes that define Andalusia.

Ultimately, the role of nature in shaping Andalusian identity is profound and multifaceted. It informs the region's agricultural practices, inspires artistic expression, and fosters a deep-seated respect for the environment. As travelers immerse themselves in the stunning vistas and rich cultural heritage of Andalusia, they will discover that the land is not just a setting for their adventures but an integral part of the stories that define this vibrant region. Understanding this relationship enriches the travel experience, inviting visitors to appreciate the soul of Andalusia through its landscapes and the people who call it home.

Chapter 2: Historical Footprints

Prehistoric Beginnings

The prehistoric era of Andalusia is a captivating tapestry woven with the threads of ancient cultures, landscapes, and human evolution. This region, situated in the southern part of Spain, is one of the richest archaeological zones in Europe, revealing a profound connection to our earliest ancestors. Rock art, discovered in caves such as those at Nerja and La Pileta, showcases the creativity and spiritual life of prehistoric communities. These artworks, dating back thousands of years, depict animals, human figures, and abstract symbols, providing insight into the beliefs and daily lives of those who roamed these lands long before recorded history.

The Neolithic period marked a significant transformation in Andalusia as communities transitioned from nomadic lifestyles to settled agricultural societies. This shift led to the establishment of some of the earliest farming villages, where the cultivation of crops and domestication of animals became central to daily life. The fertile plains of Andalusia, coupled with its diverse climate, allowed for the growth of essential crops such as wheat and barley. Travelers can explore archaeological sites like the dolmens of Antequera, which serve as a testament to the advanced understanding of architecture and communal burial practices among these early inhabitants.

As the Bronze Age unfolded, the region witnessed increased cultural complexity and interaction with neighboring civilizations. The emergence of metallurgy transformed not only tools and weapons but also social structures, as communities began to form around trade networks. The discovery of copper and bronze artifacts at sites like the Castillo de Doña Blanca reveals how these advancements facilitated economic exchanges and cultural diffusion. Travelers venturing through these historical landscapes can appreciate the remnants of this era, reflecting the ingenuity and resourcefulness of prehistoric societies in Andalusia.

The Iberians, who inhabited Andalusia during the late prehistoric and early historic periods, left an indelible mark on the landscape and culture. Their settlements, characterized by fortified hilltop structures and intricate pottery, provide a glimpse into their sophisticated way of life. The Iberian civilization was known for its skilled craftsmanship and trade relations with other Mediterranean cultures, including the Phoenicians and Greeks. As travelers explore the remains of Iberian cities such as Osuna and Castillo de Carchuna, they can gain a deeper understanding of the region's rich historical narrative and the cultural exchanges that shaped it.

The prehistoric beginnings of Andalusia set the stage for the vibrant mosaic of cultures that would follow, influencing art, architecture, and social systems. The echoes of these early societies resonate in the landscape, inviting travelers to embark on a journey through time. As you traverse the rugged mountains and serene valleys, the remnants of prehistoric life become a bridge to understanding the resilience and creativity of those who came before. This journey through Andalusia's prehistoric past not only enriches the travel experience but also fosters a profound appreciation for the deep-rooted heritage that continues to define this enchanting region.

The Roman Influence

The Roman influence on Andalusia is a defining aspect of the region's historical and cultural landscape. As one of the provinces of the Roman Empire, Hispania Baetica, which corresponds largely to modern Andalusia, was a vital center of trade, agriculture, and culture. The Romans recognized the strategic importance of this southern territory, establishing cities such as Corduba (Córdoba), Hispalis (Seville), and Malaca (Málaga) that became flourishing urban centers. The remnants of Roman architecture and engineering can still be seen throughout the region, serving as a testament to their advanced civilization.

One of the most remarkable legacies of Roman rule is the extensive network of roads that they constructed. These roads facilitated not only military movement but also trade and communication across the empire. The Via Augusta, for instance, connected the Iberian Peninsula with the rest of the Roman world, allowing goods, ideas, and cultures to flow freely. Travelers today can follow these ancient routes, exploring the remnants of Roman milestones and bridges that have withstood the test of time, offering a fascinating glimpse into the past.

The influence of Roman architecture is especially evident in the ruins of amphitheaters, temples, and baths scattered throughout Andalusia. The Roman theater in Mérida, though slightly outside the borders of modern Andalusia, is emblematic of the grand structures that once dotted the landscape. Similarly, the ruins in Itálica, near Seville, showcase impressive mosaics and the layout of a Roman city, providing insight into the daily lives of its inhabitants. These sites not only highlight Roman engineering prowess but also illustrate the cultural exchanges that took place in this vibrant region.

Religion also underwent significant transformation during Roman rule, as traditional pagan practices began to blend with early Christian beliefs. This syncretism can be observed in some of the architectural styles and artworks that emerged during this period. As churches and basilicas were built upon the foundations of Roman temples, travelers can witness the layering of history and the evolving spiritual landscape of Andalusia. This melding of cultures is a key theme in the region, offering a rich narrative of coexistence and adaptation.

In contemporary Andalusia, the Roman influence continues to shape the cultural identity of the region. Festivals, culinary traditions, and even local dialects are infused with elements that trace back to Roman customs. The annual celebration of local heritage, such as the reenactment of ancient Roman games in various towns, reflects a collective memory that honors this significant chapter in Andalusian history. For travelers seeking to understand the soul of Andalusia, exploring the Roman influence is essential for appreciating the rich tapestry of cultural and historical narratives that define this enchanting region.

The Moorish Era and Al-Andalus

The Moorish Era, which spanned nearly eight centuries, marked a transformative period in the history of the Iberian Peninsula, particularly in what is now known as Andalusia. This era began with the Umayyad conquest in 711 AD and extended until the fall of Granada in 1492. During this time, Al-Andalus emerged as a center of cultural, scientific, and economic prosperity, characterized by a unique blend of Islamic, Christian, and Jewish influences. Travelers venturing into this region today can still witness the lasting impact of this rich history through its architecture, art, and traditions.

The architectural heritage of the Moorish Era is one of the most striking features of Andalusia. Cities like Seville, Cordoba, and Granada boast stunning examples of Islamic architecture, with intricate tilework, horseshoe arches, and expansive courtyards. The Great Mosque of Cordoba, now a cathedral, stands as a testament to the architectural ingenuity of its time. The Alhambra in Granada, with its elaborate palaces and serene gardens, represents the zenith of Moorish design and continues to captivate visitors with its beauty and historical significance. These structures not only reflect the artistic achievements of the Moors but also serve as a reminder of the intricate cultural exchanges that took place during this period.

In addition to architecture, the Moorish Era was a time of remarkable advancement in various fields, including science, medicine, and philosophy. Al-Andalus became a hub for scholars who translated and preserved classical texts from ancient Greece and Rome, fostering an environment of intellectual curiosity. Figures such as Averroes and Maimonides emerged from this vibrant intellectual landscape, influencing both Islamic and European thought. Travelers can delve into this rich scholarly tradition by visiting former centers of learning, such as the University of Al-Qarawiyyin in Fez, which, while located outside Spain, represents the broader network of knowledge that flourished during this time.

The social fabric of Al-Andalus was equally diverse, with Muslims, Christians, and Jews coexisting and contributing to a shared cultural identity. This convivencia, or coexistence, allowed for the exchange of ideas, culinary traditions, and artistic expressions. Travelers can explore this multicultural heritage through local festivals, music, and culinary experiences that showcase the fusion of flavors and traditions. The annual Feria de Abril in Seville, for instance, is a vibrant celebration that highlights the region's rich history through dance, food, and traditional dress, offering a glimpse into the spirit of Andalusia that has endured through centuries.

As travelers explore the landscapes of Andalusia, they will find that the Moorish Era has left an indelible mark on the region's identity. From the breathtaking views of the Sierra Nevada mountains surrounding Granada to the sun-soaked plains of the Guadalquivir River, the natural beauty of the land complements its historical significance. The remnants of Moorish castles, such as those found in Ronda and Alcázar de Sevilla, offer a tangible connection to the past and invite visitors to reflect on the legacy of this era. In every corner of Andalusia, the echoes of the Moorish influence resonate, inviting travelers to embark on a journey through time and discover the soul of a region that continues to inspire awe and wonder.

Chapter 3: Architectural Wonders

The Alhambra: A Jewel of Granada

The Alhambra, an architectural marvel perched on the rolling hills of Granada, is a testament to the rich tapestry of history that defines Andalusia. This magnificent palace and fortress complex, originally constructed in the mid-13th century during the Nasrid dynasty, embodies a unique fusion of Islamic art and architecture. Its name, derived from the Arabic word for "red," reflects the hue of the sun-drenched walls, which glow with a warm, earthy tone at sunset. Travelers are drawn to its intricate stucco work, lush gardens, and serene courtyards, each element narrating a story of the past and inviting exploration.

As visitors approach the Alhambra, they are greeted by the stunning views of the Sierra Nevada mountains, providing a breathtaking backdrop to the historical site. The entry into the Alhambra is marked by the imposing gates that lead to the Nasrid Palaces, a series of interconnected rooms and courtyards that showcase the pinnacle of Moorish architecture.

Highlights include the iconic Patio de los Leones, featuring a fountain surrounded by twelve marble lions, and the intricately decorated Sala de los Embajadores, where the sultans once held court. Each space is adorned with elaborate tile work and calligraphy, reflecting the artistic achievements of the era.

Beyond the palatial splendor lies the Generalife, the summer palace and gardens of the Nasrid rulers. This serene retreat offers a stark contrast to the formal grandeur of the Alhambra's palaces, with its cascading fountains, fragrant flowers, and shaded pathways. Travelers wandering through the Generalife will find themselves enveloped in a world of tranquility, where the sounds of water and the scents of blooming jasmine create a sensory experience unlike any other. The gardens not only served as a place of leisure but also represent the Islamic ideal of paradise on earth, inviting contemplation and connection with nature.

The historical significance of the Alhambra extends beyond its architectural beauty; it stands as a symbol of the cultural exchanges that took place during the Reconquista. After the Christian conquest of Granada in 1492, the Alhambra became a focal point of fascination and inspiration for artists and writers, influencing the Romantic movement in the 19th century. Literary figures such as Washington Irving penned works that romanticized the Alhambra, embedding it deeply in the cultural consciousness of Spain and beyond. Today, it continues to inspire countless travelers and artists, serving as a bridge between past and present.

Visiting the Alhambra is not merely an exploration of a historical site; it is an immersion into the soul of Andalusia itself. The blend of cultures, the stories etched into its walls, and the breathtaking landscapes surrounding it create an unforgettable experience. For travelers seeking panache in their journeys, the Alhambra offers an unparalleled opportunity to connect with the essence of a region that has captivated hearts and minds for centuries. As they stroll through its corridors and gardens, visitors are reminded that the Alhambra is more than just a monument; it is a living testament to the enduring spirit of Andalusia.

The Mezquita of Córdoba

The Mezquita of Córdoba, a stunning monument of Islamic architecture, stands as a testament to the rich cultural tapestry of Andalusia. Originally constructed in the 8th century as a mosque, it reflects the grandeur of the Umayyad dynasty, showcasing an intricate design that marries both function and artistry. The structure's vast prayer hall, adorned with over 850 columns made of marble, onyx, and jasper, creates an awe-inspiring atmosphere that transports visitors back to a time when Córdoba was the intellectual and cultural capital of the Islamic world. This architectural marvel not only highlights the ingenuity of its creators but also serves as a symbol of the coexistence of different cultures throughout history.

As travelers approach the Mezquita, they are greeted by its striking façade, a blend of Moorish and Renaissance architectural styles. The original entrance, with its elaborate horseshoe arches and intricate tile work, invites exploration. Once inside, the play of light through the stained glass windows casts a kaleidoscope of colors across the interior, enhancing the spiritual ambiance of the space. The mosque's unique double arches, a hallmark of Moorish design, allow for an expansive yet intimate setting, creating a sense of infinity that enchants visitors. Each architectural detail invites contemplation, revealing the artistic vision that has captivated generations.

Following the Reconquista in 1236, the Mezquita was converted into a Catholic cathedral, known as the Cathedral of Our Lady of the Assumption. This transformation introduced a series of Baroque chapels and altars that coexist with the mosque's original features, creating a dialogue between two faiths. The juxtaposition of the Islamic and Christian elements within the same space symbolizes the complex history of Andalusia and the layers of cultural integration that have shaped the region. Travelers can marvel at the juxtaposition of the grand Renaissance altar and the exquisite mihrab, each telling its own story of devotion and artistry.

In addition to its architectural significance, the Mezquita of Córdoba serves as a cultural hub that hosts various events throughout the year. From concerts to art exhibitions, the mosque-cathedral continues to be a lively center of community life, bridging the past and present. Visitors are encouraged to engage with the ongoing narrative of this historic site, which remains a focal point for discussions on cultural heritage, preservation, and interfaith dialogue. The Mezquita not only stands as a monument of architectural beauty but also as a living testament to the enduring spirit of Córdoba.

For travelers seeking to immerse themselves in the essence of Andalusia, the Mezquita of Córdoba is an unmissable experience. Its rich history, breathtaking design, and the harmonious blend of cultures offer a unique perspective on the region's past and present. As one wanders through its halls, there is a palpable sense of connection to the myriad of stories that have unfolded within these walls. The Mezquita invites exploration and reflection, making it a profound destination for those who wish to understand the soul of Andalusia.

The Giralda of Seville

The Giralda of Seville stands as a striking emblem of the city's rich history and architectural grandeur. Originally built as a minaret for the Great Mosque of Seville during the 12th century, this remarkable structure showcases the intricate artistry of Almohad architecture. Rising to a height of 104 meters, the Giralda is not only a symbol of Islamic heritage but also a testament to the city's cultural evolution following the Reconquista. It is an essential stop for any traveler eager to understand the layers of history that define Andalusia.

Visitors to the Giralda are often captivated by its unique design, which seamlessly blends Islamic and Christian elements. The original minaret featured a series of ornate arches and a smooth, tapering silhouette, while the addition of a bell tower in the 16th century transformed it into a Christian landmark. The iconic statue known as "El Giraldillo," which crowns the tower, represents faith and is a striking figure that can be seen from various points around the city. This fusion of styles not only reflects the city's diverse past but also illustrates the adaptability of its architecture over centuries.

The journey to the top of the Giralda is an integral part of the experience, offering an opportunity to ascend the ramp that was designed for the muezzin to call the faithful to prayer. Unlike traditional staircases, the gentle incline allows for a more leisurely ascent, making it accessible to a wide range of visitors. As travelers climb, they are rewarded with breathtaking views of Seville's skyline, including the sprawling rooftops of the historic Santa Cruz neighborhood and the majestic outline of the Cathedral of Seville. Each step offers a new perspective on the city's landscape, underscoring the interconnectedness of its history and architecture.

Surrounding the Giralda, the Plaza del Triunfo provides a vibrant space that enhances the experience of visiting this iconic monument. The plaza is a hub of activity, filled with street performers, local vendors, and travelers. Here, one can soak in the atmosphere of Seville, where the essence of Andalusian culture comes alive. The presence of the Cathedral, the Royal Alcázar, and the Archivo General de Indias nearby further enriches the experience, inviting visitors to explore the stories of the past that converge in this dynamic area.

In conclusion, the Giralda of Seville is not just an architectural marvel; it is a symbol of the city's enduring spirit and a reflection of its historical complexities. For travelers seeking to immerse themselves in the soul of Andalusia, a visit to this iconic tower offers a deeper understanding of the region's cultural tapestry. As they gaze out over the city from its heights, they can appreciate the intricate dance of history that continues to shape Seville, making each visit to the Giralda a personal journey through time.

Chapter 4: The Flamenco Spirit

Origins of Flamenco

Flamenco, a passionate and expressive art form, has its roots deeply embedded in the rich cultural tapestry of Andalusia. Its origins can be traced back to the fusion of various influences that converged in this southern region of Spain. The historical context of Andalusia, marked by centuries of cultural exchanges due to trade, conquest, and migration, played a significant role in shaping the unique characteristics of flamenco. The region's diverse population, including Moors, Jews, and Gypsies, contributed to a melting pot of musical styles, rhythms, and traditions that ultimately gave rise to flamenco as we know it today.

The early forms of flamenco emerged in the 18th century, primarily among the Romani people, who settled in Andalusia. Their distinct musical practices, combined with local folk traditions, created a foundation for the flamenco genre. The use of guitar, handclaps, and percussive footwork became hallmarks of this art form, emphasizing both rhythm and emotion. The intersection of these elements allowed flamenco to evolve, and it quickly gained popularity beyond the Romani community, attracting the attention of various social classes and communities throughout Andalusia.

As flamenco continued to develop, it began to incorporate influences from different musical styles, including Arab, Jewish, and even African rhythms. The Moorish occupation of Spain left a lasting impact on the region's music, introducing complex rhythms and modal scales that enriched flamenco's sound. Additionally, the Jewish presence contributed to the emotive vocal styles seen in flamenco singing, known as "cante." This blending of traditions created a dynamic and multifaceted genre that resonated with the struggles and passions of the Andalusian people.

Flamenco's rise to prominence was not just due to its musical richness but also to its cultural significance. It became a means of expression for marginalized communities, particularly during difficult periods in Spanish history. The art form encapsulated the joys, sorrows, and resilience of the Andalusian spirit. As flamenco gatherings, or "juergas," became popular, they served as communal spaces where people could connect through music and dance, reinforcing social bonds and cultural identity.

By the 20th century, flamenco had transitioned from a regional folk art to a celebrated performance art, gaining recognition worldwide. The establishment of flamenco festivals and dance schools helped to elevate its status and attract international audiences. Today, flamenco is not only a symbol of Andalusian culture but also a testament to the region's ability to blend diverse influences into a cohesive and powerful art form. Travelers exploring Andalusia can immerse themselves in this vibrant tradition, experiencing firsthand the passion and history that have shaped flamenco as a living expression of the soul of the region.

Key Influences and Styles

The cultural tapestry of Andalusia is woven from a rich history of influences that have shaped its identity over centuries. From the early civilizations of the Iberians and Celts to the profound impact of the Moors, each group left an indelible mark on the region's architecture, language, and customs. The Moorish conquest in the

8th century introduced a sophisticated blend of art, science, and philosophy, evident in the intricate designs of structures like the Alhambra and the Great Mosque of Córdoba. This period saw the flourishing of knowledge and culture, creating a legacy that continues to resonate in contemporary Andalusian society.

One cannot discuss the influences in Andalusia without acknowledging the profound impact of the Catholic Reconquista in the 15th century. As the Moors were expelled, a wave of Christian architecture emerged, juxtaposing the ornate Islamic motifs with Gothic and Renaissance styles. The result is a unique architectural landscape where cathedrals rise alongside palaces, each telling a story of the region's complex past. Cities like Seville and Granada exemplify this fusion, where visitors can witness the seamless interplay between different artistic expressions that characterize Andalusia's historical narrative.

The flamenco tradition, a cornerstone of Andalusian culture, embodies the region's eclectic influences. Rooted in the diverse backgrounds of the Romani people, Moorish rhythms, and Jewish melodies, flamenco is a passionate expression of the Andalusian spirit. Travelers can experience this vibrant art form in intimate venues throughout the region, where the interplay of guitar, singing, and dance evokes the emotional depth of Andalusian life. Such performances serve as a living testament to the cultural syncretism that defines this part of Spain, inviting spectators to immerse themselves in its dynamic history.

Andalusia's culinary landscape is another reflection of its diverse influences, showcasing flavors and techniques that have evolved over centuries. The region's cuisine is characterized by a harmonious blend of Mediterranean ingredients, Arabic spices, and traditional Spanish recipes. Dishes such as gazpacho, paella, and tapas reveal the historical exchanges between cultures, offering travelers a taste of the past through the palate. Markets filled with fresh produce and local delicacies provide a sensory experience that highlights the importance of food in Andalusian culture, making every meal a journey through history.

Artistic expressions in Andalusia, from painting to literature, further illustrate the region's diverse influences and styles. Renowned artists such as Pablo Picasso and Diego Velázquez drew inspiration from their Andalusian roots, contributing to a vibrant artistic heritage that continues to inspire. The literary works of writers like Federico García Lorca encapsulate the essence of Andalusia, weaving themes of passion, nature, and identity into their narratives. For travelers, exploring the artistic landscape of Andalusia is an invitation to engage with the profound cultural legacies that shape the region, enriching their understanding of its soul.

Experiencing Flamenco in its Birthplace

Experiencing flamenco in its birthplace offers travelers an unparalleled glimpse into the cultural heart of Andalusia. Originating in the Andalusian region, flamenco is not just a dance but a profound expression of emotion, history, and identity. To truly appreciate its essence, one must immerse themselves in the vibrant cities where flamenco was born, notably Seville, Jerez de la Frontera, and Granada. Each city presents its unique twist on this art form, influenced by the diverse cultures that have settled in the region over centuries, including Moorish, Jewish, and Romani traditions.

In Seville, the birthplace of flamenco, visitors can explore the historic neighborhoods of Triana and Santa Cruz, where the sounds of guitar, clapping, and passionate voices fill the air. Attending an authentic flamenco show in an intimate tablao allows travelers to witness the raw emotion and technical prowess of the performers up close. In these venues, the fusion of guitar rhythms, soulful singing, and fervent dance creates an electric atmosphere that captivates audiences. The performers often share personal stories through their art, making each performance a unique experience that resonates deeply with the audience.

Jerez de la Frontera, known for its sherry production, is another essential stop for flamenco enthusiasts. The city hosts an annual flamenco festival that attracts artists and fans from around the world, showcasing the depth and variety of flamenco styles. Here, travelers can participate in workshops, learning from seasoned dancers and musicians, immersing themselves in the technical aspects of the dance. The city's flamenco clubs, or peñas, provide a more local experience, where one can enjoy impromptu performances and engage with the community that keeps this art form alive.

Granada, with its stunning backdrop of the Sierra Nevada mountains, adds yet another layer to the flamenco experience. The Sacromonte neighborhood is famous for its cave performances, where artists perform in natural acoustics that enhance the intensity of their expression. The combination of flamenco with the picturesque views of Alhambra creates a magical setting that enriches the experience. Visitors can wander through the narrow, winding streets, soaking in the vibrant atmosphere, and discovering the deep connections between the landscape and the emotional narratives expressed through flamenco.

To truly understand flamenco is to appreciate it as a living, breathing art form that evolves while remaining deeply rooted in its history. Travelers who venture into the heart of Andalusia not only witness the captivating performances but also engage with the stories and traditions that shape this cultural heritage. Whether through a riveting show in Seville, a lively festival in Jerez, or an intimate cave performance in Granada, experiencing flamenco in its birthplace allows travelers to connect with the soul of Andalusia and the emotional power of its people.

Chapter 5: Culinary Journeys

Traditional Dishes of Andalusia

Andalusia, a region steeped in history and culture, boasts a culinary landscape that reflects its diverse influences. Traditional dishes of Andalusia are a testament to the rich agricultural heritage and the fusion of flavors brought by various civilizations over centuries. The Mediterranean climate, with its sun-drenched plains and fertile soil, yields an abundance of fresh ingredients that are the foundation of Andalusian cuisine. Travelers seeking to immerse themselves in the local culture will find that food is not merely sustenance but an experience that connects them to the land and its people.

One of the most iconic dishes of Andalusia is gazpacho, a refreshing cold soup that embodies the essence of summer. Made primarily from ripe tomatoes, peppers, cucumbers, garlic, olive oil, and vinegar, gazpacho is a vibrant blend of flavors that showcases the region's agricultural bounty. Traditionally consumed during the hot months, this dish is often enjoyed as a starter or a light meal. Each family has its own variation, adding ingredients like bread or herbs, making it a versatile staple that travelers can discover in countless local eateries.

Another culinary gem is salmorejo, a thicker cousin of gazpacho originating from Córdoba. This dish features a creamy blend of tomatoes, bread, olive oil, and vinegar, served chilled and often garnished with hard-boiled eggs and jamón serrano. The simplicity of salmorejo belies its rich flavor and satisfying texture, making it a favorite among locals and visitors alike. As travelers explore the charming streets of Córdoba, sampling salmorejo at a local tavern offers a taste of tradition and an opportunity to engage with the region's culinary heritage.

Fried fish, or pescaíto frito, is a beloved dish along the Andalusian coast, particularly in cities like Málaga and Cádiz. This dish typically features small, whole fish, lightly battered and fried to golden perfection. Served with a wedge of lemon, pescaíto frito is often enjoyed as a tapa, providing a casual and social dining experience. The coastal towns celebrate this dish during local festivals, where travelers can savor the flavors of the sea while soaking in the vibrant atmosphere.

Lastly, no exploration of Andalusian cuisine would be complete without mentioning the rich array of stews and paellas. Dishes like pisto, a ratatouille-like vegetable stew, and the famous seafood paella highlight the region's agricultural and maritime resources. These hearty meals are often prepared for communal gatherings, reflecting the Andalusian spirit of hospitality. Travelers are encouraged to seek out local markets and family-run restaurants to experience these traditional dishes, allowing them to savor the flavors of Andalusia while connecting with the region's culinary history.

The Influence of the Mediterranean

The Mediterranean Sea has long been a cradle of civilization, shaping the cultures and landscapes of the regions that border it. In Andalusia, this influence is profoundly woven into the fabric of daily life, architecture, cuisine, and even the rhythms of social interactions. The coastal towns and cities, from Seville to Málaga, reflect a unique blend of cultures that have thrived in the shadow of the Mediterranean. This subchapter explores how the sea has influenced Andalusian identity and heritage, creating a rich tapestry that continues to attract travelers seeking to understand the essence of this remarkable region.

The geographical position of Andalusia along the Mediterranean coast has made it a historical crossroads for diverse civilizations, including the Phoenicians, Romans, and Moors. Each of these cultures left an indelible mark on the landscape, contributing to a distinctive architectural style that merges Islamic, Gothic, and Renaissance elements. Iconic structures such as the Alhambra in Granada and the Alcázar in Seville showcase intricate tile work, lush gardens, and elaborate water features that reflect the Mediterranean's affinity for beauty and harmony. This confluence of influences not only tells the story of Andalusia's past but also captivates visitors with its aesthetic appeal.

The Mediterranean climate, characterized by hot, dry summers and mild, wet winters, has also played a pivotal role in shaping the agricultural practices of the region. The fertile lands of Andalusia produce an abundance of olives, citrus fruits, and grapes, which have become staples of the local diet and economy. Travelers can indulge in the rich flavors of traditional dishes such as gazpacho, paella, and a variety of tapas that highlight the region's culinary heritage. This gastronomic journey is further enhanced by the Andalusian tradition of communal dining, where meals are enjoyed in the company of family and friends, reflecting the Mediterranean spirit of connection and celebration.

The influence of the Mediterranean extends beyond the physical and cultural landscape; it is deeply embedded in the artistic expressions of Andalusia. Flamenco, a passionate dance and music form, draws inspiration from the rhythms of the sea and the diverse cultures that have graced the region. The haunting melodies and intricate footwork are a testament to the emotional depth and cultural fusion that characterize Andalusian art. Travelers can immerse themselves in this vibrant scene by attending performances in local tablaos, where the energy of the Mediterranean ambiance enhances the experience and offers a glimpse into the soul of Andalusia.

Finally, the Mediterranean is not just a backdrop; it is a living entity that shapes the lifestyle and worldview of the Andalusian people. The sea serves as a source of inspiration and a means of livelihood, with fishing and tourism playing vital roles in the local economy. Coastal towns like Tarifa and Nerja are gateways to stunning beaches and outdoor activities, inviting travelers to engage with the natural beauty of the Mediterranean. As one explores the coastline, they encounter a rhythm of life that emphasizes relaxation, enjoyment, and a profound appreciation for nature, encapsulating the essence of Andalusian culture and its enduring connection to the Mediterranean.

Wine and Tapas: A Cultural Experience

Wine and tapas are at the heart of Andalusian culture, offering travelers a unique glimpse into the region's rich history and social fabric. Andalusia's climate and geography have fostered the cultivation of grapes, leading to a vibrant winemaking tradition that dates back centuries. Renowned for its sherry, particularly from the Jerez region, Andalusia showcases a variety of wines that reflect the local terroir. The production methods, often passed down through generations, emphasize the connection between the land and its people, making each glass a story waiting to be told.

Pairing wine with tapas is not merely a culinary practice; it is an essential part of socializing in Andalusia. Tapas, which originated as small plates served alongside drinks, have evolved into a diverse array of dishes that range from simple olives to elaborate seafood preparations. This tradition encourages sharing and conversation, fostering a communal spirit among friends and strangers alike. As travelers indulge in these delightful bites, they partake in a ritual that reflects the Andalusian way of life, where food and drink serve as a bridge between cultures and generations.

The experience of enjoying wine and tapas is deeply embedded in the local customs of Andalusian cities. In Seville, the bustling tapas bars are filled with laughter and animated discussions, while in Granada, the practice of offering a complimentary tapa with each drink creates a welcoming atmosphere for visitors. Each city boasts its own specialties, with local wines often paired with regional dishes, providing an opportunity for travelers to explore the nuances of Andalusian gastronomy. It is not uncommon for locals to recommend their favorite pairings, adding a personal touch to the culinary journey.

Travelers can immerse themselves in this cultural experience by participating in wine and tapas tours, which often include visits to local wineries and markets. Such tours provide insight into the winemaking process, allowing visitors to meet the passionate artisans behind the bottles. Sampling wines alongside expertly prepared tapas not only tantalizes the palate but also enriches the understanding of how regional ingredients influence flavor profiles.

These experiences create lasting memories and foster a deeper appreciation for the culinary heritage of Andalusia.

As travelers enjoy wine and tapas, they engage with a culture that values tradition, community, and the simple pleasures of life. The act of sharing food and drink transcends mere sustenance, embodying the spirit of Andalusia itself. For those seeking to connect with the essence of this vibrant region, indulging in its wine and tapas is an unmissable experience that highlights the interplay of history, landscape, and social interaction, leaving a lasting imprint on the heart and soul of every visitor.

Chapter 6: Festivals and Celebrations

Semana Santa: A Deeply Religious Tradition

Semana Santa, or Holy Week, is a profoundly significant event in Andalusia, celebrated with fervor and devotion across the region. This religious tradition, which commemorates the passion, death, and resurrection of Jesus Christ, showcases the deep-rooted Catholic heritage that permeates Andalusian culture. Each year, thousands of pilgrims and visitors flock to cities like Seville, Málaga, and Granada to witness the breathtaking processions, where elaborate floats adorned with religious icons are carried through the streets by cofradías, or brotherhoods. The processions are not merely events; they are a spiritual journey that evokes a sense of reverence and reflection.

The intricacies of Semana Santa are revealed through the painstaking preparation that begins months in advance. Brotherhoods organize their processions, often with a history that stretches back centuries. Each brotherhood has its own distinct identity, colors, and patron saint, contributing to the rich tapestry of the celebrations. The float bearers, known as costaleros, train rigorously to carry the heavy pasos, or floats, showcasing intricate sculptures and religious imagery. The dedication and commitment of these individuals highlight the communal spirit that defines Semana Santa, making it a collective expression of faith and artistry.

As the week progresses, the streets of Andalusia transform into an open-air theater of devotion. The sound of drums and the haunting notes of saetas, traditional flamenco songs sung in homage to the processions, resonate through the air. Spectators line the streets, their faces illuminated by the flickering light of candles held by penitents dressed in traditional robes and pointed hoods, a practice that dates back to the Middle Ages. This visual spectacle is not only an aesthetic experience but also a profound reminder of the sacrifices made and the stories of redemption that lie at the heart of the Christian faith.

The emotional impact of Semana Santa is palpable, as participants and onlookers alike engage in a shared experience of reflection and mourning. The processions often evoke tears and quiet contemplation, creating an atmosphere that transcends the ordinary. The solemnity is counterbalanced by moments of celebration, as the resurrection of Christ on Easter Sunday brings jubilant festivities. This blend of sorrow and joy encapsulates the essence of Semana Santa, reinforcing its significance as a transformative experience for both the faithful and the curious traveler seeking to understand the spiritual depth of Andalusia.

For travelers wishing to immerse themselves in this deeply religious tradition, Semana Santa offers a unique glimpse into the soul of Andalusia. Visitors are encouraged to participate respectfully, observing the rituals and traditions that unfold. Engaging with locals, attending pre-processional events, and savoring traditional foods associated with the week can enhance the experience. Whether witnessing the solemnity of the processions or participating in the vibrant celebrations of Easter Sunday, travelers will leave with a profound appreciation for the cultural and spiritual heritage that Semana Santa embodies.

Feria de Abril: The Heart of Seville

Feria de Abril, or the April Fair, is a vibrant celebration that captures the essence of Seville and embodies the spirit of Andalusia. Held two weeks after Easter, this annual event transforms the city into a kaleidoscope of colors, sounds, and traditions. The fairgrounds, known as the Real de la Feria, come alive with elaborately decorated tents, each serving as a social hub for families and friends. The air is filled with the scent of traditional tapas, the sound of flamenco music, and the sight of locals dressed in traditional attire, making it a feast for the senses that draws both residents and visitors alike.

At the heart of the Feria is the rich cultural heritage that defines Seville. The festival originated in the 19th century as a livestock fair but has since evolved into a celebration that showcases Andalusian customs and traditions. Visitors can witness the artistry of flamenco dancers, the intricate designs of traditional costumes, and the skilled craftsmanship of local artisans. The atmosphere is charged with excitement as people gather to enjoy live music, participate in dance competitions, and indulge in the region's culinary delights. Each element of the Feria reflects the deep-rooted history and passion of the Andalusian people.

The Feria de Abril is not just a spectacle; it is also a time for community and connection. Families prepare for months, creating their own casetas, or tents, where they welcome friends and share meals. These tents, often adorned with colorful fabrics and lights, serve as a gathering place for laughter, storytelling, and celebration. The bond between locals is palpable, making the Feria a unique opportunity for travelers to immerse themselves in the warmth and hospitality of Andalusian culture. Engaging with locals during the fair provides insights into their traditions and fosters a sense of belonging that transcends the typical tourist experience.

For travelers, experiencing the Feria de Abril offers a chance to participate in a living tradition. Visitors are encouraged to dress in traditional Andalusian attire, allowing them to blend in and fully embrace the festivities. The fair also features thrilling activities such as horseback riding, amusement rides, and flamenco performances, ensuring there is something for everyone to enjoy. Whether wandering through the lively streets, savoring the various tapas on offer, or dancing the sevillanas, travelers can create lasting memories during this enchanting celebration.

As the sun sets over Seville, the Feria transforms into a magical wonderland illuminated by thousands of lights. The joyful atmosphere reaches its peak with late-night parties, where music and laughter echo throughout the fairgrounds. The Feria de Abril is more than just a festival; it is a heartfelt expression of Andalusian identity, a celebration of life, and a testament to the enduring spirit of the people of Seville. For those seeking to understand the soul of Andalusia, experiencing the Feria is an unforgettable journey into its heart.

Local Festivals: A Journey Through Community

Local festivals in Andalusia serve as vibrant expressions of culture and community, drawing travelers into a world where tradition and celebration intertwine. Each festival is a window into the soul of the region, showcasing its rich history, artistic heritage, and the deep-rooted customs that define the Andalusian way of life. From the lively streets of Seville during Feria de Abril to the solemn processions of Semana Santa, these events reveal the diverse tapestry of local identity and collective memory.

Feria de Abril, or the April Fair, is one of Andalusia's most iconic festivals, celebrated in Seville with a fervor that captivates visitors. The fair transforms the city into a colorful spectacle of flamenco dresses, horse parades, and lively casetas (marquees) where locals and travelers alike indulge in tapas and sherry. As the sun sets, the fairgrounds pulse with music and dance, inviting all to join in the revelry. This festival not only highlights the region's culinary delights but also serves as a reminder of the importance of community, as families and friends gather to celebrate their heritage with pride.

Semana Santa, or Holy Week, offers a stark contrast to the exuberance of Feria de Abril, presenting a more solemn yet deeply spiritual experience. Throughout Andalusia, particularly in cities like Seville and Malaga, elaborate processions take place, featuring ornate floats carrying religious icons. The atmosphere is charged with emotion as participants don traditional robes and carry candles through the streets, creating a powerful sense of unity and reflection. Visitors are encouraged to engage respectfully with this profound tradition, which illustrates the significance of faith in shaping Andalusian culture.

In smaller towns and villages, local festivals often celebrate patron saints or seasonal harvests, providing a more intimate glimpse into Andalusian life. Festivals such as the Romería de El Rocío in Huelva draw thousands of pilgrims who embark on a journey to pay homage to the Virgen del Rocío. This celebration blends religious devotion with community bonding, as participants travel on horseback or in colorful caravans, singing and dancing along the way. These local festivals allow travelers to experience authentic customs and build connections with residents, fostering a sense of belonging even in unfamiliar surroundings.

The myriad festivals of Andalusia not only serve as entertainment but also play a crucial role in preserving cultural heritage and fostering community spirit. As travelers immerse themselves in these celebrations, they gain a deeper understanding of the region's history and the values that underpin its community life. Each festival offers a unique narrative, reflecting the resilience, creativity, and warmth of the Andalusian people, inviting all who visit to partake in the rich experience that is central to the soul of Andalusia.

Chapter 7: Natural Landscapes

The Sierra Nevada: A Mountain Escape

The Sierra Nevada mountains, a majestic range that rises dramatically in southern Spain, offer travelers an unparalleled escape into nature's grandeur. This stunning landscape, characterized by its towering peaks, deep valleys, and diverse ecosystems, serves as a natural barrier between the Mediterranean climate of the coastal regions and the arid interior of the country. The Sierra Nevada is not just a geographical marvel; it is also a rich tapestry of history, culture, and adventure waiting to be explored. For those seeking both tranquility and exhilaration, this mountain range is a sanctuary where the soul can rejuvenate amidst breathtaking vistas.

The highest peak in the Sierra Nevada, Mulhacén, stands at an impressive 3,479 meters, making it the tallest mountain in mainland Spain. The ascent to Mulhacén is a rewarding challenge that attracts hikers and climbers from around the world. The trail winds through ancient pine forests and alpine meadows, offering stunning views of the surrounding landscapes. As travelers trek higher, they are enveloped by the crisp mountain air and the scent of wild herbs, while the sound of distant waterfalls adds to the serene ambiance. Reaching the summit, one is greeted with a panorama that stretches across the horizon, revealing the intricate beauty of the Andalusian landscape below.

Beyond the exhilarating climbs, the Sierra Nevada is a treasure trove of biodiversity. The region is home to numerous endemic species, both flora and fauna, some of which can only be found in this unique environment. The delicate balance of ecosystems here supports rare plants, such as the Sierra Nevada bluebell, and wildlife, including the endangered Spanish ibex. Nature enthusiasts will find endless opportunities for exploration, whether it's birdwatching, botany, or simply immersing themselves in the tranquility of the natural surroundings. Each season brings its own charm, from the vibrant colors of spring wildflowers to the crisp, snow-laden beauty of winter.

Culturally, the Sierra Nevada is steeped in history, with ancient trails that once connected villages and facilitated trade. The influence of the Moors can still be felt in the architecture and traditions of the region. Traditional whitewashed villages, such as Capileira and Pampaneira, nestle in the foothills, offering a glimpse into the past. These charming hamlets invite travelers to wander their narrow streets, sample local delicacies, and enjoy the warm hospitality of the residents. The rich tapestry of culture is interwoven with the stunning natural backdrop, creating a unique experience that resonates deeply with visitors.

For those who seek adventure, the Sierra Nevada offers a plethora of activities throughout the year. In addition to hiking and climbing, the region is perfect for skiing and snowboarding in the winter months, with the Sierra Nevada Ski Resort providing excellent facilities. Mountain biking, paragliding, and horseback riding are also popular among thrill-seekers. Yet, even for those who prefer a more leisurely pace, the mountains provide ample opportunities for relaxation and reflection. Whether it's soaking in the beauty of a sunset over the peaks or enjoying a quiet moment by a mountain stream, the Sierra Nevada is truly a mountain escape that nurtures the spirit and enriches the soul.

The Costa del Sol: Sun and Surf

The Costa del Sol, stretching along the southern coast of Spain, is a captivating blend of sun-drenched beaches, vibrant culture, and rich history. This region, with its enviable climate boasting over 300 days of sunshine a year, has become a haven for travelers seeking both relaxation and adventure. The shoreline is dotted with charming towns and bustling resorts, each offering unique experiences that reflect the essence of Andalusia. From the glistening Mediterranean waters to the rugged mountains that rise just inland, the Costa del Sol is a landscape that beckons exploration.

The beaches of the Costa del Sol are among its most enticing features. With golden sands and crystal-clear waters, they provide an idyllic setting for sunbathing, swimming, and a variety of water sports. Popular spots like Marbella and Torremolinos are renowned for their lively atmospheres, where visitors can indulge in beachside dining, vibrant nightlife, and numerous recreational activities. For those seeking a quieter escape, hidden coves and picturesque beaches such as Playa de Burriana in Nerja offer serene alternatives, allowing travelers to unwind amidst stunning natural beauty.

Beyond the allure of its beaches, the Costa del Sol is steeped in history, with remnants of its rich past visible in its architecture and cultural offerings. Towns like Ronda and Mijas showcase a blend of Moorish and Spanish influences, reflected in their narrow streets, whitewashed buildings, and historic landmarks. Visitors can explore the ancient bullring in Ronda or wander through the charming streets of Mijas, where artisanal shops and local eateries provide a taste of authentic Andalusian life. The region's historical sites, including the Alcazaba in Almería and the Roman ruins of Marbella, offer a glimpse into the diverse civilizations that have shaped the landscape over centuries.

The Costa del Sol is also a paradise for outdoor enthusiasts, with opportunities for hiking, golfing, and exploring the natural parks that dot the region. The Sierra de las Nieves, a UNESCO Biosphere Reserve, offers stunning trails that wind through lush forests and dramatic landscapes, perfect for those looking to immerse themselves in the natural beauty of Andalusia. Additionally, the coastline is ideal for surfing, especially in areas like El Palmar and La Barrosa, where waves attract surfers from around the globe. These activities not only provide an adrenaline rush but also allow travelers to appreciate the stunning vistas that characterize this part of Spain.

Culinary experiences along the Costa del Sol are as rich and varied as its landscapes. The region is known for its fresh seafood, tapas bars, and delightful local wines, particularly the sweet Malaga wine. Dining along the coast often features dishes like grilled sardines, fried fish, and the famous paella, all enjoyed with the backdrop of the shimmering sea. Markets such as the Atarazanas Market in Málaga showcase the vibrant local produce, inviting travelers to taste the flavors of Andalusia. For those who wish to delve deeper into the culinary scene, cooking classes and food tours offer the chance to learn about traditional recipes and techniques, enhancing the overall travel experience.

The White Villages: Hidden Gems of Andalusia

The White Villages, or "Pueblos Blancos," are a collection of traditional towns nestled in the mountainous regions of Andalusia, renowned for their stunning whitewashed buildings and breathtaking landscapes. These villages, characterized by narrow cobblestone streets, vibrant flower-filled balconies, and an air of timeless charm, offer travelers a glimpse into Andalusia's rich cultural heritage. Each village has its own unique story and architectural style, reflecting the influences of Moorish and Christian legacies. Exploring these hidden gems provides an opportunity to experience the authentic essence of Andalusian life beyond the more tourist-heavy cities.

Ronda, one of the most famous of the White Villages, is perched dramatically atop a deep gorge and is known for its stunning bridge, the Puente Nuevo, which connects both sides of the ravine. The town's history dates back to Roman times, and visitors can explore ancient ruins alongside the impressive 18th-century architecture. Ronda serves as a gateway to the Sierra de Grazalema Natural Park, making it an ideal base for travelers seeking outdoor adventures such as hiking, birdwatching, and horseback riding. The village's vibrant local culture is showcased through its traditional festivals, such as the annual Feria de Pedro Romero, celebrating the region's bullfighting heritage.

Grazalema, another picturesque village, is famous for its stunning natural scenery and lush surroundings. Known as one of the rainiest places in Spain, it boasts a unique ecosystem that supports diverse flora and fauna. The village itself is a labyrinth of winding streets, where the white houses are adorned with colorful flowers and intricate wrought-iron details. Grazalema is also recognized for its artisanal crafts, particularly in the production of woolen goods, which travelers can find in local shops. The nearby Natural Park of Sierra de Grazalema offers stunning hiking trails, including routes that lead to the breathtaking Garganta Verde gorge.

Arcos de la Frontera is often described as a jewel of the White Villages, with its dramatic cliffside location overlooking the surrounding countryside. The town is characterized by its blend of Moorish and Gothic architecture, evident in the intricate details of its churches and palaces. A stroll through the historic center reveals captivating viewpoints and charming plazas, where travelers can savor local delicacies in inviting tapas bars. Arcos is particularly famous for its wine production, inviting visitors to explore local bodegas and enjoy tastings of the region's exquisite sherries.

Finally, the village of Mijas offers a unique blend of traditional Andalusian charm and modern amenities. Perched on a mountainside, Mijas features stunning views of the Mediterranean coastline and is known for its donkey taxis, an amusing and eco-friendly way to navigate the village's steep streets. The quaint whitewashed buildings are decorated with vibrant ceramics and art, showcasing the creativity of local artisans. Mijas also boasts beautiful walking trails that meander through the surrounding hills, providing travelers with a peaceful escape and opportunities for exploration in the stunning Andalusian landscape. Each of these White Villages not only captivates the eye but also tells a story of the enduring spirit and rich history of Andalusia.

Chapter 8: Cities of Andalusia

Seville: The Cultural Capital

Seville stands as a vibrant testament to Andalusia's rich cultural heritage, making it an essential destination for travelers seeking to immerse themselves in the region's history and art. Known for its stunning architecture, lively atmosphere, and deep-rooted traditions, Seville offers a unique blend of influences that reflect its diverse past. From the Moorish legacy evident in the Alcázar to the Gothic grandeur of the Cathedral, the city's landmarks tell stories of centuries of cultural exchange and evolution, inviting visitors to explore the layers of history that shape its identity.

The annual Feria de Abril, a celebration of flamenco, local cuisine, and traditional costumes, highlights Seville's role as a cultural capital. This vibrant festival transforms the city into a kaleidoscope of color and sound, attracting locals and tourists alike. The rhythmic clapping of castanets, the twirling dresses of flamenco dancers, and the tantalizing aroma of tapas create an immersive experience that showcases the city's passion for life and community. Attending the Feria provides travelers with an opportunity to engage with Seville's spirited culture, offering a taste of the traditions that have been passed down through generations.

Art lovers will find a haven in Seville, as the city boasts an impressive array of museums and galleries. The Museo de Bellas Artes, housed in a former convent, features an extensive collection of Spanish paintings, including works by masters such as Murillo and Zurbarán. Contemporary art also thrives in Seville, with spaces like the CAAC (Centro Andaluz de Arte Contemporáneo) showcasing innovative exhibitions that reflect current cultural dialogues. This duality of historical and contemporary art allows travelers to appreciate the city's artistic evolution while engaging with its dynamic present.

Seville's culinary scene further enhances its status as a cultural capital. The city's tapas bars serve as social hubs, where locals and visitors can savor a variety of small dishes, from jamón ibérico to gazpacho. Exploring the culinary landscape not only satisfies the palate but also provides insight into the communal aspect of Andalusian culture. Cooking classes and food tours allow travelers to delve deeper into the culinary traditions that define Seville, creating lasting memories through shared meals and stories.

As the sun sets, Seville transforms into a magical realm, with its streets illuminated by soft lights and the sounds of laughter and music filling the air. The city's vibrant nightlife, characterized by lively flamenco shows and bustling plazas, offers an enchanting glimpse into the local way of life. Travelers can enjoy evenings spent in intimate tablaos, where the passionate performances of flamenco artists capture the essence of Andalusian spirit. This dynamic interplay of history, art, cuisine, and nightlife solidifies Seville's place as the cultural capital of Andalusia, inviting all who visit to discover the soul of this captivating city.

Granada: A Fusion of History and Modernity

Granada, a city nestled at the foot of the Sierra Nevada mountains, is a captivating blend of historical grandeur and contemporary vibrancy. This Andalusian gem is most renowned for the Alhambra, a UNESCO World Heritage site that stands as a testament to Moorish architecture and artistry. The intricate tile work, lush gardens, and breathtaking palaces of the Alhambra evoke a sense of nostalgia for a bygone era, offering travelers a glimpse into the rich tapestry of Islamic culture that flourished in the region during the 13th and 14th centuries. As one wanders through its corridors, the echoes of poets and philosophers resonate, creating an ambiance that is both enchanting and reflective.

Beyond the Alhambra, Granada's historic neighborhoods, such as the Albaicín and Sacromonte, showcase the city's diverse cultural influences. The Albaicín, with its narrow, winding streets and whitewashed houses, reflects the legacy of the Moors, while the Sacromonte district, famous for its cave dwellings, reveals the deep-rooted traditions of flamenco, an art form that embodies the spirit of Andalusia. Travelers can immerse themselves in the local culture by exploring artisan shops, enjoying traditional tapas, or attending a flamenco performance, where the passion and rhythm bring the city's vibrant history to life.

Granada also embraces modernity, evident in its contemporary architecture and artistic endeavors. The city has seen a resurgence in innovative design, with structures like the Science Park and the new metro line blending seamlessly into the urban landscape. These developments not only enhance the city's functionality but also serve as a canvas for artistic expression. Local galleries and street art projects illustrate the dynamic relationship between Granada's past and present, inviting travelers to appreciate how modern influences coexist with historical significance.

Culinary exploration in Granada further exemplifies this fusion of history and modernity. The city is home to a flourishing gastronomic scene that marries traditional Andalusian recipes with contemporary culinary techniques. From the bustling markets where local produce is sold to upscale restaurants offering innovative dishes, the flavors of Granada reflect its diverse cultural heritage. Travelers can indulge in a meal featuring classic ingredients like olive oil, fresh vegetables, and spices, all while enjoying the backdrop of the city's stunning architecture.

In essence, Granada stands as a living testament to the harmonious coexistence of history and modernity. The city invites travelers to journey through its past while engaging with its present, creating an experience that is both enriching and invigorating. As visitors meander through its streets, they are not merely observing a city; they are participating in an ongoing narrative that celebrates Andalusia's cultural richness and historical depth, making Granada a must-visit destination for those seeking to connect with the soul of this remarkable region.

Córdoba: The City of Tolerance

Córdoba, once the capital of the Islamic Caliphate in the 10th century, stands as a testament to a unique historical period marked by cultural exchange and religious tolerance. This vibrant city, nestled along the banks of the Guadalquivir River, showcases an intricate tapestry of influences from various civilizations, including Romans, Visigoths, and Moors. Travelers who wander through its narrow, winding streets will encounter an array of architectural marvels that reflect this rich heritage, making Córdoba a living museum of tolerance and coexistence.

One of the most striking symbols of this harmonious past is the Great Mosque of Córdoba, or La Mezquita. Originally built as a mosque, it was later converted into a cathedral following the Reconquista. The mesmerizing arches and intricate mosaics within the mosque illustrate the artistic prowess of Islamic architecture, while the Christian additions highlight the city's evolution. Visitors can marvel at the seamless blend of architectural styles, a physical representation of the city's history of religious intermingling. This site invites reflection on the past and offers a powerful reminder of what can be achieved when different cultures come together.

Córdoba's historical significance is further accentuated by its Jewish Quarter, known as the Judería. This area is characterized by its narrow alleyways, whitewashed buildings, and the ancient synagogue, one of the few that remains in Spain. The Judería serves as a poignant reminder of the Jewish community that thrived in Córdoba during the Middle Ages. Here, travelers can explore a rich cultural legacy, including the traditions, customs, and contributions of the Jewish people to the city's development. The coexistence of Jewish, Christian, and Muslim communities contributed to a vibrant intellectual atmosphere, fostering advancements in philosophy, science, and the arts.

In addition to its architectural and historical gems, Córdoba is home to a lively cultural scene that continues to celebrate its diverse heritage. Festivals throughout the year, such as the Feria de Córdoba and the Festival of Patios, showcase the city's communal spirit and artistic expression. The Festival of Patios, in particular, is a vivid display of color and creativity, as locals open their beautifully decorated courtyards to visitors, reflecting the communal pride and hospitality that epitomize Córdoba's character. These events invite travelers to engage with the living culture of Córdoba, where the spirit of tolerance and celebration continues to flourish.

Córdoba's legacy of tolerance extends beyond its historical and cultural landmarks; it serves as an inspiration for contemporary society. In an increasingly polarized world, the city stands as a beacon of hope, illustrating the potential for harmony among diverse communities. For travelers seeking to understand the essence of Andalusian identity, Córdoba provides a profound exploration of how past civilizations can inform present values of acceptance and coexistence. By immersing themselves in the city's rich history and vibrant culture, visitors can appreciate Córdoba not only as a destination but as a symbol of what it means to embrace diversity.

Chapter 9: Spiritual Journeys

The Path of Santiago de Compostela

The Path of Santiago de Compostela, known as the Camino de Santiago, is a profound pilgrimage that has attracted travelers for centuries. This ancient route, leading to the shrine of Saint James in Santiago de Compostela, is steeped in history and spirituality. The Camino offers not only a physical journey through the stunning landscapes of northern Spain but also an opportunity for personal reflection and connection with the rich cultural heritage of the region. For travelers seeking to immerse themselves in the essence of Andalusia, walking part of this route reveals the region's unique blend of history, art, and natural beauty.

Starting in Andalusia, the Camino is marked by diverse terrains, from rolling hills to rugged mountains, each step echoing the footsteps of countless pilgrims who have walked before. The journey often begins in towns like Seville or Córdoba, where travelers can explore majestic cathedrals, Moorish architecture, and vibrant local markets. The significance of these cities lies not only in their historical landmarks but also in the stories they tell—stories of faith, resilience, and the meeting of cultures that have shaped Spain's identity. As travelers set out on the path, they are invited to engage with this rich tapestry of history that defines Andalusia.

As the Camino winds its way through picturesque villages and stunning landscapes, travelers are treated to a sensory feast. The olive groves, vineyards, and sunflower fields create a vibrant backdrop, while the aroma of local cuisine wafts through the air. Each stop along the way offers a chance to savor traditional Andalusian dishes, such as gazpacho and tapas, reflecting the region's culinary heritage. Engaging with local communities adds depth to the journey, as travelers encounter artisans, farmers, and fellow pilgrims, sharing stories and creating connections that transcend language and culture.

The spiritual dimension of the Camino cannot be overlooked. For many, the pilgrimage is a time for introspection and renewal. The rhythm of walking, combined with the serene landscapes, encourages a meditative state, allowing travelers to contemplate their own lives and aspirations. The experience of reaching Santiago de

Compostela is a culmination of not just the physical journey but also the emotional and spiritual growth that occurs along the way. This pilgrimage fosters a sense of belonging, drawing travelers into a wider community of seekers who share a common goal.

In conclusion, the Path of Santiago de Compostela is more than just a journey through Andalusia; it is an exploration of the soul. The combination of breathtaking scenery, rich cultural experiences, and personal reflection makes this pilgrimage a transformative adventure. For those who venture along the Camino, each step taken is an invitation to discover not only the beauty of the landscape but also the deeper meaning of their own journey through life. Embracing the spirit of the Camino allows travelers to connect with Andalusia in a way that resonates long after the journey has ended.

The Influence of Religion on Art and Culture

The interplay between religion and art in Andalusia is a testament to the region's rich cultural tapestry, woven from threads of various faiths. The Islamic period, which lasted for several centuries, left an indelible mark on the artistic expressions that define Andalusian heritage today. The intricate geometric patterns, arabesques, and calligraphy found in mosques and palaces reflect a profound spiritual significance, illustrating the belief that art should evoke a sense of the divine. Notably, the Alhambra in Granada stands as a pinnacle of this artistic expression, where every tile and archway serves both an aesthetic and spiritual purpose, inviting reflection and awe.

Following the Reconquista, the integration of Catholicism into the artistic landscape brought forth a new era of creativity, characterized by a fusion of Moorish elements with Baroque and Renaissance styles. Churches and cathedrals, such as the magnificent Seville Cathedral, showcase this blending through their towering spires and intricate altarpieces. Artists like Francisco de Zurbarán and Bartolomé Esteban Murillo emerged, creating works that conveyed religious narratives while also embracing the sensuality and dynamism of the Baroque. This period not only transformed religious spaces but also allowed for the exploration of human emotion within sacred themes, establishing a unique Andalusian identity.

The influence of Judaism also permeated Andalusia's artistic and cultural landscape, particularly during the period of coexistence known as La Convivencia. Jewish communities contributed significantly to the intellectual and artistic life of cities like Toledo and Córdoba, where the synthesis of Jewish, Christian, and Islamic thought flourished. This cultural exchange is evident in the architectural styles of synagogues, which often mirrored the aesthetics of mosques and churches. The legacy of Jewish craftsmanship and scholarship continues to resonate, as seen in contemporary artistic expressions that draw from this historical interplay.

In modern times, the echoes of religious influence can be observed in festivals and cultural practices throughout Andalusia. Events such as Semana Santa (Holy Week) exemplify the deep-rooted connection between faith and artistic expression, showcasing elaborate processions adorned with intricate pasos, or floats, that depict scenes from the Passion of Christ. These celebrations not only serve as a spiritual observance but also as a platform for artistic creativity, where craftsmanship in sculpture, painting, and music converge to create a profound cultural experience for both locals and travelers.

As travelers explore the diverse landscapes of Andalusia, the influence of religion on art and culture becomes evident in every corner. From the stunning architecture of historic sites to the vibrant traditions that shape contemporary life, the intertwining of faith and creativity reveals a deeper understanding of the region's soul. By appreciating this intricate relationship, visitors can gain insight into the values and beliefs that have shaped Andalusia for centuries, enriching their journey through this captivating land.

Sacred Sites and Pilgrimages

Sacred sites and pilgrimages in Andalusia hold a profound significance that transcends mere tourism, offering travelers a glimpse into the region's rich tapestry of spirituality and historical devotion. From ancient temples to revered shrines, these locations resonate with centuries of faith, culture, and community. The sacred landscapes of Andalusia invite visitors to explore not only the physical beauty of the land but also the deep spiritual connections that have shaped its identity. Each site embodies a story, reflecting the diverse influences that have converged in this southern Spanish region.

One of the most prominent sacred sites is the Cathedral of Seville, built upon the remnants of a grand mosque. This architectural marvel is not only a testament to Gothic design but also a symbol of the intricate history of religious coexistence that defines Andalusia. The Giralda tower, originally constructed as a minaret, offers breathtaking views of the city and has become an essential stop for pilgrims and tourists alike. The cathedral's interior, adorned with chapels and altars, serves as a reminder of the enduring nature of faith and the artistry that accompanies it.

The pilgrimage to Santiago de Compostela, while not exclusive to Andalusia, draws many travelers through the region as they journey along the Camino de Santiago. This ancient route, which has seen countless pilgrims over the centuries, provides a unique opportunity for personal reflection and connection to history. As travelers traverse the varied landscapes—from the rolling hills of the Sierra de Grazalema to the sun-drenched plains of the Guadalquivir—they encounter charming villages and hospitable locals who share in the spirit of the pilgrimage. The experience fosters a sense of camaraderie among pilgrims, uniting them through shared purpose and discovery.

The annual pilgrimage to the Sanctuary of Our Lady of the Rocío, known as El Rocío, stands out as one of Andalusia's most vibrant spiritual events. Each spring, thousands of devotees from across the region converge upon the small village of Almonte to honor the Virgen del Rocío. This lively celebration blends religious fervor with cultural traditions, featuring colorful processions, song, and dance. Travelers who partake in this pilgrimage not only witness the devotion of the participants but also immerse themselves in the rich folklore and communal spirit that defines Andalusian culture.

Exploring sacred sites and participating in pilgrimages in Andalusia allows travelers to engage with the region's profound spiritual heritage. Whether visiting ancient cathedrals, walking historic routes, or joining in time-honored celebrations, each experience enriches one's understanding of Andalusia's identity. These journeys through sacred landscapes provide travelers with the opportunity to reflect on their own beliefs, connect with the past, and appreciate the enduring power of faith in shaping the human experience. The soul of Andalusia, intertwined with its sacred traditions, invites all who visit to embark on a journey that transcends the physical and enters the realm of the spiritual.

Chapter 10: Modern Andalusia

Urban Development and Preservation

Urban development and preservation in Andalusia represent a delicate balance between progress and heritage. As travelers seek to explore the region's vibrant cities, they encounter a rich tapestry of architectural styles that reflect centuries of cultural influences. From the Moorish designs of Córdoba to the Renaissance splendor of Seville, each city tells a story of its past while adapting to the needs of modern life. Urban development initiatives often aim to enhance infrastructure, improve public spaces, and accommodate the growing influx of visitors, all while ensuring that the unique character of Andalusian cities is maintained.

One of the key challenges in urban development is the preservation of historical sites. In Andalusia, countless monuments and neighborhoods are designated as UNESCO World Heritage Sites, which brings both opportunities and responsibilities. Planners must navigate complex regulations that protect these invaluable assets while integrating them into the fabric of contemporary urban life. This requires innovative approaches to urban design that respect the historical context, such as creating pedestrian-friendly zones that allow visitors to experience the beauty of these sites without compromising their integrity.

The role of local communities in urban development cannot be overlooked. Residents often play a crucial role in advocating for preservation efforts, sharing their knowledge and passion for their heritage. Engaging local voices in the planning process ensures that development aligns with the community's identity and values. Travelers can witness this dynamic in action, as many cities host forums and workshops where citizens collaborate with urban planners to voice their concerns and suggestions. This participatory approach fosters a sense of ownership and pride among residents, enriching the travel experience for those who visit.

Sustainable development practices are increasingly becoming a focal point for urban planners in Andalusia. As cities grapple with the effects of climate change and urban sprawl, initiatives aimed at sustainability are gaining traction. The promotion of green spaces, the use of eco-friendly materials in construction, and the preservation of traditional farming practices are just a few examples of how modern development can coexist with historical preservation. Travelers exploring Andalusia can appreciate these efforts, as they contribute to the overall quality of life in the region while maintaining its historical essence.

Ultimately, the relationship between urban development and preservation in Andalusia is a reflection of the region's broader cultural identity. As cities evolve, they do so while honoring their past, creating a unique blend of old and new. For travelers, this offers a captivating experience, allowing them to witness firsthand the ongoing dialogue between history and modernity. By exploring urban spaces that have managed to retain their soul amidst change, visitors can gain a deeper appreciation for the richness of Andalusian culture and the resilience of its communities.

The Impact of Tourism

The impact of tourism in Andalusia is multifaceted, influencing its economy, culture, and environment. As one of Spain's most visited regions, Andalusia draws millions of travelers each year, eager to explore its rich history, diverse landscapes, and vibrant traditions. This influx of visitors has become a significant driver of economic growth, providing employment opportunities in various sectors, including hospitality, transportation, and local crafts. The revenue generated from tourism not only supports local businesses but also contributes to the funding of public services and infrastructure improvements, enhancing the quality of life for residents.

However, the effects of tourism extend beyond economic benefits. The cultural landscape of Andalusia has been shaped by its visitors, who bring diverse perspectives and experiences that enrich local traditions. Festivals, culinary offerings, and artisanal crafts have evolved through the interplay between local customs and global influences. This cultural exchange fosters a sense of pride among locals, who are encouraged to preserve their heritage while also embracing new ideas. Nevertheless, there is a delicate balance to maintain, as excessive tourism can threaten the authenticity of cultural expressions and lead to the commodification of traditions.

Environmental considerations are another critical aspect of tourism's impact in Andalusia. The region's stunning natural landscapes, including the Sierra Nevada mountains and the Costa del Sol coastline, attract nature enthusiasts and beachgoers alike. While tourism can promote environmental awareness and conservation efforts, it also poses challenges such as habitat degradation, pollution, and resource depletion. Sustainable tourism practices are paramount to ensure that the landscapes that define Andalusia are preserved for future generations. Initiatives aimed at reducing the ecological footprint of tourism, such as promoting eco-friendly accommodations and responsible travel behaviors, are essential to mitigate these impacts.

The interaction between tourists and locals plays a vital role in shaping the region's social fabric. While tourism can foster connections and intercultural dialogue, it can also lead to tensions and misunderstandings. Residents may feel overwhelmed by the sheer number of visitors, resulting in concerns about overcrowding and a loss of local identity. Engaging with the community through authentic experiences, such as local tours or cooking classes, can help bridge the gap between travelers and residents. Such interactions not only enrich the travel experience but also promote mutual respect and understanding.

In conclusion, the impact of tourism in Andalusia is profound and complex, encompassing economic, cultural, environmental, and social dimensions. As travelers embark on their journeys, they hold the power to influence the region positively by supporting local businesses, respecting cultural practices, and advocating for sustainable tourism. By approaching their travels with mindfulness and appreciation for the local way of life, visitors can contribute to the preservation of Andalusia's soul, ensuring that its rich history and breathtaking landscapes continue to inspire future generations.

A Vision for the Future

As travelers seek to explore the rich tapestry of Andalusia, a vision emerges that intertwines this region's storied past with its promising future. The allure of Andalusia lies not only in its breathtaking landscapes and historic cities but also in the vibrant culture and traditions that continue to evolve. This vision for the future embraces a sustainable approach to tourism, one that honors the heritage of the land while fostering innovation. By prioritizing responsible travel practices, visitors can immerse themselves in authentic experiences that respect the natural environment and local communities.

One key aspect of this vision is the promotion of eco-tourism, which emphasizes the importance of preserving Andalusia's diverse ecosystems. The region boasts stunning national parks, picturesque coastline, and rolling olive groves that deserve protection. Future travelers will find themselves drawn to activities such as hiking, birdwatching, and agritourism, which allow them to engage with the landscape while minimizing their ecological footprint. By supporting local businesses that prioritize sustainability, visitors can contribute to the preservation of the region's unique flora and fauna.

Cultural preservation also plays a crucial role in shaping the future of Andalusia. The rich heritage of flamenco, traditional crafts, and culinary arts must be safeguarded and celebrated. Initiatives that connect travelers with local artisans and cultural practitioners can enhance the visitor experience while ensuring that these traditions are passed down through generations. Workshops, performances, and food tours provide opportunities for deeper engagement, fostering a mutual appreciation between travelers and the local communities that welcome them.

The advancement of technology presents another avenue to enrich the travel experience in Andalusia. Digital platforms can facilitate connections between travelers and local guides, ensuring that visitors discover hidden gems beyond the typical tourist path. Virtual reality experiences can enhance historical understanding, allowing travelers to visualize the past while walking through ancient ruins or wandering the streets of historic towns. By harnessing technology, the future of travel in Andalusia can become a harmonious blend of innovation and authenticity.

Ultimately, a vision for the future of Andalusia invites travelers to become stewards of the region's remarkable heritage. By embracing sustainable practices, supporting local cultures, and utilizing technology wisely, visitors can contribute to a thriving ecosystem that benefits both people and the planet. As travelers embark on their journeys through Andalusia, they are not merely observers but active participants in a narrative that continues to unfold, ensuring that the soul of this enchanting land remains vibrant for generations to come.

Made in United States
Cleveland, OH
22 February 2025

14590287R00030